PERSPECTIVES

George Bruce

PERSPECTIVES

Poems 1970 - 1986

First published 1987
Aberdeen University Press
A member of the Pergamon group

© George Bruce 1987

The publisher acknowledges subsidy from the Scottish
Arts Council towards the publication of this volume

British Library Cataloguing in Publication Data

Bruce, George, 1909-
   Perspectives: collected poems 1970-1986.
   I. Title
   821'.914   PR6052.R7/
   ISBN 0—08—035062—3

PRINTED IN GREAT BRITAIN
THE UNIVERSITY PRESS
ABERDEEN

To

ELIZABETH

CONTENTS

ACKNOWLEDGEMENTS

Acknowledgements for the hitherto uncollected poems are due to *Akros, Lines Review, The Scottish Review, Scottish Poetry* (6-9), *A Scottish Poetry Book, A Second Scottish Poetry Book, Life and Work, Orbis, A Scottish Childhood, Natural Light, The Living Doric, Birds, Spirit* (U S A), *The Literary Review* (U S A), *Interim* (U S A), *Meanjin* (Australia).

PROLOGUE   VISIONS

OLD MAN AND SEA

Nightfall — was it still out there?

The rusty, white iron gate trembled
as it opened to the path to the sea
down by the ramblers, unseen,
no scent, for the salt had taken over.
With all my fearing childhood in it
I hear it growling in the dark. Ahead
from where the marram grass meets sand,
between me and the slapping water — a figure:
he stands square-shouldered staring
into that nothing.
                              How many mornings
when the silvered horizon promised,
giving hope for that day
or when the mist stood impenetrable,
or when the sky burst and the sea met it,
I thought, he waited, thought I knew him,
might approach, touch him, claim him for kin,
he who stood his ground for us all,
but there is no reckoning in this matter.
Square-shouldered I stood looking into that nothing.

BETWEEN

Always as we lifted our eyes
from that dust which told us of our deaths
it was there waving, juicy, yet wavering
through waves of heat: and we were forever
approaching it, and forever watering
our spirits so that we did not know
we were little other than dry bones.
Now, though we had died then, having
many times reached that place where
our spirits and eyes told us green
grass grew: though scientists and doctors
had simple final explanations that

what we saw we merely imagined, did so
for the sake of sustaining our mortal bodies
as if they were immortal, still
with wilful obstinacy, stupidity, we believed,
totally convinced there was a place for us
where the lark above sang in her blue sky,
and below meadows sweet with running water.

Then they set the computers on us to produce
the final evidence that we were predictably computed,
and that the final figures were on our brows.
There was no escaping the verdict.
We drew a circle in the sand.
Within it we, the last of the believers in
that seeming state — between — would
perish, die, not for lack of sustenance,
but through the now accepted rationale
that all could be accounted by the tool
that plotted the graph of our being,
reducing, with absolute precision, to formulae,
the excited tremblings of what we called spirit.

Then one observed:
'The circle itself is an abstraction.'

IN THE BEGINNING
The Visitor finds Eden in Australia

Suddenly they addressed themselves to him.

The kookaburra gave its heartless laugh
for him. 'Curra-wa, curra-wong', sang
the pied currawong. Twenty sulphur cockatoos
cursed above from the white gum's branch.
Bush parrots, rosellas, king parrots, even
a lyre bird, presented their credentials.
A coiled yellow-black snake uncoiled.
The curiosities of nature were on display.
Trees grew out of dust, lifting themselves
light-green and airy into the steady blue.
The sun hoisted itself into the northern sky.

She walked among the falling gold in late
autumn sun, and not a stitch on her,
ran, jumped under the tumbling fall
that sparkled from its source in desert.
The koalas, of course, clung to his
god-like presence, adoring as ever
those who assumed worship as their due.

When he turned his back did
the scenario, so carefully scripted,
collapse? Did the scene-shifters
go about their business removing
the flimsy structures, spitting
on raw hands, the show being over,
or is all as it was after his darkness
fell, waiting for another?

        . . . And in Scotland

He had come this way before
when the little fish of childhood,
inches long only, and quicksilver,
but pink beneath the dorsal fin,
moved with superb locomotion,
and the green crab, awkward, scuttled
its side-wise motion under a rock,
when the beaches offered see-through
fan shells, the size of his pinkie nail
and fabulous whorled shells that echoed
with hushings vast unknowable oceans.
'Write it doon,' said the whorled shell
into his lug. 'Pit it doon for your Da.'
Write it down for mother, for father,
for all the forked kind, the big heads
with eyes that read. 'Scrieve it,
scrieve it!' scraiched the gulls.
'As Duns Scotus said,' said the Prof.
'objects may possess individualities
peculiar to themselves. This thisness,
haecceitas, should be a central interest
in your papers. Evidences are expected
as witness to your conclusions.'

The Witness

Witness to what? Each page continued
to make its proposals to him that signs
should be put on it, that these
might be picked up by unknown eyes —
an assumption that the deadly rains
had not already destroyed all witnesses.
Certainly there was an impression of continuity:
a cockatoo squawked across the leaden sky,
a snake disturbed the waters that rose
above the floor-boards of the room.
But no planes, no comforting sound
of a combustion engine. Of that solace,
the accompaniment to the routine engagements
which had made civilisation possible,
nothing. No receiver of signs, then no
necessity. Yet perhaps as that last bird
sped between the boughs uttering harsh cries,
as the snake's body looped and unlooped
in muddy waters, there was the last requirement
to find that impossible speech which sang
of the creation that was.
                In the dark
gathering in that upper room, he looked out
at the swaying, cracking branches — sound:
sight — possibly a twinkle in the leaves:
then in the perceiver light in the eyes.
The sweet word rolled from the tongue:
'Light. Light. Light.'

CHESTNUT TREE — JUNE 1970*

This year the candles came late.
Waiting for June they burned in the sun.
At night they lit the moon that lit
the destroyed graves of the children of Peru.

Candles — do you burn with hate or love
or with nothing at all? The priests
lit candles for the dead of Peru,
walking into the ruined night for love.

The candles erect on the plangent leafage,
dance a ritual dance in the Scottish wind.
They incite the children to tumble,
to ride their bicycles without hands,

to ridicule an old man passing by,
to swing on the plunging branches in the wind.
The children shout for joy.
They disappear into the body of the tree.

At night the tree is a torch.
Its bare branches are ash.
A bird flies into the sky.

* The date of an earthquake in Peru

G B's SEA SYMPHONY

The conductor with his white carnation,
one hand on the steel rail of the rostrum,
the other, baton raised to the blue sky,
conducts the waves. They roll towards him,
endlessly pushing their white sibilance,
while the ocean gathers its symphonic mass.

We watched from our cracking deck chairs,
listening to the swelling adagio. At allegro
ripples pizzicatoed at the black coat tails.
He swings into a crescendo, ripping the sky
with a stroke. From their backsides on dry land
seat-holders glimpse the frenetic point of his up-beat.

The prom-strolling dainties, yellow-teethed old men,
groovy, geared groups, holiday haymakers on the blistered
beach, saw nothing, heard nothing, while the North Sea
sent its blue word over our conductor. In a trough
we saw the head turn, the circus white-wash face
with the jelly lips, the gaga stare. No encores.

You read this score once. The beach attendant stacks
the chairs. Five pence a time to watch the breakers
whiten in the sun. Tomorrow the next of kin mounts
the rostrum, raises his baton; they are the lemming
kind, ridiculous, mad; belief swims in their heads
that the earth makes music for them, for us.

FROM THE SHORELINE

MOON MEN

Back from the moon
on the white officered
ship, the moon rocket captain
shook hands with the top people,
known by their gold braid.

In the sea village of Cairnbulg
John shook hands with
the fisherman, Jeems Buchan,
who had got back from
the moon-controlled Yarmouth fishing,

while south having taken time off
to inspect the Codex Siniaticus
in the British Museum.

Jeems Buchan put his foot
on the grass at his doorstep
took thirty steps to the sea
for seventy years.

Gilbert, his son,
stood on the slippery deck too.
The conditions made for
adaptation to novelty.

He was expert in the use
of radar and the lot,
became a naval lieutenant,
returned from the war to fish.

John stayed at the croft
that looked to the sea
kept a bull.
Jeems kept a cat.

Little puss, little puss,
hunting a sparrow,
looking for salt fish
between earth smell and sea smell,

little puss, little puss,
as you pad between
brine and bull,
earth trembles, sea shudders.

In the night
John hears the bull thump
at the post,
Jeems the sea's roar.

In the night
a gale couped John's rick,
took Jeems' yawl clean
from beach to grass.

No fishing
for three days,
then flat calm
and a low mist.

The white lifted
from the sea's face.
An arctic tern
exploded the silver.

Jeems said,
'We're for off.'

As specified he collected
rocks and moondust,
carried out the complicated
measurements and operations,
noted the effects of asteroids,
meteorites, cometary materials,
set up instruments, checked gauges,
returned (as programmed) to the machine,

arrived, having accomplished
marvels of precision, celebrated,
at the ordained place and time,
home on the unknowable earth.

Sit by me, little puss,
sit by me, little cat,
who looks for the remains
of fish.

Look wisely and run from
the trembling sea.

On the white plain
he lifts his limbs in slow motion
moving towards the edge
of the disc that recedes
at the pace of his steps.

The occasion lacks gravity
as he rolls on lunar business.
With full military honours,
at attention, vertical, he plants
The Stars and Stripes to canned music.

Home, a dog barked in the night.
In the Spring the crocuses came again.

AND DID THOSE FEET ...

Black in the morning sun, Sunday boots
athwart swinging shoulders, feet pad white
across three miles of sand, upright men
bound for the kirk, who swung off Kinnaird
for fish. Necessity, custom, and in their heads
Christ calling his disciples, sinners who'd
boozed last night, a few taken illicit sex,
most held to their known purpose for life,
resolved, drowned in tears, howled at
by evangelist Jock Troup, washed by him
in the blood of the lamb. Christ have mercy!
Monday — John Gatt, who'd done it all,
locked to the desk in his balancing act,
has no ministers, nor booze, nor grace in his mind.

SEA MEN

I
'God in the wave!' Joe bawled as it rose
and shut out the sky. How! How? —
when the swing took the boat to his death.
No words in that waste. Black she foundered.
The Lily, her curt moment stretched out in
wind-wail, sea-moan and a wrecked moon.

The cliff house waits in the long dark;
nothing given away about the life,
that must have been, must be there
still in the dark that moved
while the wind blurted about
the stone corners that stood on stone.
Inside the place awaiting return
her world stops, blazes and cries.

II

Spewed out of the sea we crawled in the dark.
Hung nets enmeshed, creosote in cans, tarred
ropes coiled — we smelled our way like animals.
At dawn we struggled to the door and saw
the long, low light greying the horizon.
Salt tingled our eyes to life. Our soft
bodies felt again the rocks that bled us.

Set this down in a hand that shakes.
Each knowledge requires respect —
Smell tar, creosote, wood and salt air.

DEATH OF AN OLD, FAT SEAMAN

Round man on the empty crude oil drum
With your back to your mentor ocean,
Twelve miles in your tipsy yawl you'd come
To settle for, sing for, line for your portion
Of fish, for thirty years supported
The flaunting seas with a legend —
O rotund porpoise! 'Indestructible', reported,
Fixed in space without a wrinkle to portend
Age. As you rat-a-tat fat hands on your drum,
Squat Bhudda, inscrutable to tourists, dumb,
You're hauled heavenwards, strung up at the turn
Of tide, caught in the bare light of a winter sun,
And float in the air like your simple tune.
At night I see you bellying the full moon.

CATCH

For Alexander Scott, poet,
on his return from Greece,
loaded

You, Alex, went to the Aegean,
came home with a shining shot,
clean, unmarked fish.

I shot my nets thirty miles
East of North off Kinnaird,
came home with spents,

the rest torn bellies.
The dogs had got them.
Too late in the season.

That's what legends do,
purify the seas.
They're in short supply here.

OIL MEN

In memory of William Burns, R.S.A., (1921-1972)

The silver darlings had gone black,
rotting at the gills, the spermatazoa
on the wane; propulsion of energy
from below the North Sea bed,
a shot in the arm for a dying society.
Looking with green eyes
into the now recorded depth
I spotted the new squid
whose dirt's consumed by
homonculi-on-wheels hellbent,
while I would plunge headlong
into another unknown.

16

William Burns took other soundings.
A Glasgow man, practical, he
piloted a plane in the war, then flew
one to help him see the face of Scotland
abstract; settled for Aberdeen,
Art Lecturer, gave up to paint only.
To see better he flew over north-east
ports, studied spatulate piers,
geometric blocks that would concede nothing,
nor were asked by his art. He put
in the rectangle of his canvases
trawler keels, rusted plates, seams caulked
with red-lead, boat rudders that nudged,
awkward propellors, tarred planks, ropes,
white-washed wall, bollards — his canvas
a scrap-heap for forms that had long resisted
salt air and the gale. Stumpy kirk towers,
fishermen's block houses at odds with weather
came together in blobs and stabs. Lumps of paint
patched his square — his sea-town picture,
his sea-town spotted from his plane,
gone over with meticulous eye to bring
back the life that lies in wait in objects
men used to combat sea, and in the spaces
between artefact, sea and air. He made sorties,
piloted his plane on the edge of mind to see.

All over again I hear through his paint the boom
of the foghorn that howled in my child-nights.
Then it juddered the window frames set in granite.
My childhood rises from his cold look.
I heave in a mist. The story begins again,
hauling itself in dark and silver.
                              Keel over — he keeled
when once more he went on survey into his last mist.
He left his findings for the rabid few, who
(against all the blank minds taking their gain)
hold to that other.

THE RETURN

Salt on the lips and the sea unseen,
unheard; the air swinging in the head,
sheer light breaking in a shuttered room,
a torrent, the senses alerted at each
moment — this freshness remembered.

Our kind's productivity deal takes over —
the dead gull's wings weighted with oil,
plastic cleansols rule the waves,
the waves returning faeces to the shore.

Hidden in a dip in sand dunes, the wind
beaten back, sea-sound a murmur, a shelter,
where the sand loses itself in soil,
thyme and forget-me-not. Our cold
summer sun makes this a place again.

HOUSE WITH BACK-GARDEN

Our granite house
by the sea — never
out of its roaring or
shushing or hacking cough —
stood steady as any rock.

A good house with good people
in it: who looked after it,
and us. Everything there
was in its right place,
except us boys, of course,
though we knew where
we ought to be.

The way to the back green
was through the big trellised
gate. It wobbled open
when pushed or kicked
which we did. We would

TWO TOGETHER

The moon ripens in their eyes
on the silk of water. As two walk
in themselves as if in each other
the terrible entry is being written.
The sea gives up its dead.
They lie on black beaches
in the squalor of our night and day.

ALPHA AND OMEGA

Out of the inchoate
walking simply on moonlit sands
she came with a formal look

she to him   he to her
her to him   he to she

she composes herself placing
a lock of hair to flow
from neck to breast, turning
from him to sea.

On the beach short arm vertical
his fist squeezes an apple dry.
Its tears run into the shitten sea.

GULLS AND FULMAR PETRELS

Voracious it tore to rags skin and
flesh, herring in the barrel, fed
till its belly ballooned, but weighted,
trapped, so, constrained by wood, hinges
of flapping wings could not operate.
Gulls lumber in the air anyway,
while fulmars, stiff-winged, plane,
flip from cliff edge tidy, or rise
in an air-stream effortless —
a-poise, the Platonic bird itself,
the bright bird belonging to all
the wild airs, not submitting, but riding
all ease and gain in storm, high
or low shadowing frothing breakers,
or down skimming wave trough —
a delicate ghost, a spirit soundless,
an implication of an absolute
wrested from (denied by) the destined dark.

WORDS ON BEACH

Went to a stony beach to look for agates,
found none but came back with bags of words,
agates, chrysophates, pure crystals, carnelian,
as many as I wanted and much easier to carry;
took them home and began to polish them,
cracks and impurities in them too.

G B ON THE ROCKS

The facts of time sit on my balding head,
while the permutations of water affront the rock,
water day and night on it. Speculation will not
alter its longevity, nor mine. I consult my drying skin.
Curious that in these circumstances we sing,
while fate drowns the precious young,
trips up old friends, damages the innocent.

THE STONES OF IONA AND COLUMBA

They define themselves rarely
in the walls of the abbey, each
inviting attention as it shapes
in the mind, pink, grey, blue.

So through the glass of sea
on the white bed each stone,
insisting on its difference, presents
itself for the first time,

surprising us with the shock of light
and with the knowledge that it,
like God, has never been seen,
but with love a little known.

The sea pitches. The boat is thrown
on the stony beach. The cliffs echo.
A thousand years ago or more he
picked up green translucent pebbles.

Still they are strange to us. It is enough
the stones stay.

BOY AND COD'S HEAD

The grammar lesson. *Macbeth* as specimen.
'There is no speculation in those eyes.'
The line jumps from the page: gets lost.
Lines are for peerie fish, podlies, codlins.
Macbeth — a play. I play football. Sand blows
through the grasses of the football pitch
by the sea, the cemetery on the other side.
The fog settles down — sea smell, sea sound.
On the spit of sand, bleached white, a skull,
rabbit's, sand sifting through the cavities,
the bone structure a palace for life once,
where the dance began, the leap, the twist,
the scuttle to be safe, now safe in sea's cycle
with thin fan shells, buckies, whorls,
and the pink dried back shuffled off the crab.
At my feet a cod's head chopped off
its fish body, cast overboard, spewed out
with guts, entrails blood, reject of man
and sea, a violation of nature.
'There is no speculation in those eyes.'

THE DESERT

AND

OTHER MORALITIES

ON THE ROADS

Little children
walk
in their bones
on the roads.

Hump backed
wi her creel
the auld wife cried:
'Herrin. Herrin!'

An the skipper said
tae the auld wife:
'There's ower mony herrin
in the warld. Pit them

back til the ocean.'
And she did.
'Ower mony herrin
in the watter.

There's nae eneuch bellies
in the warld tae feed.
Gae back tae the sea,
Ye auld wife.'

She cam oot the sea
and she went back
intil't cryin:
'Herrin. Herrin!'

An the deid herrin floatit
on the watter.
Says the man that kens:
'Stop huntin thae herrin.

There's nae eneuch herrin
in a' the seas
tae feed thae folk
on the roads.'

Dust in a dry wind.
Hard in soft mouths.

THE DESERT
For Hugh MacDiarmid

I
POSTCARD
(Photo of Yasar Arafat, Nasser and King Hussein)

Nice photo — all smiles but
the middle one's dead. The one
on the right, the King — he swore never
to shake the hand of him on the left;
he's the guerilla, commando, freedom-fighter,
and *he* never, never, never to cease from
fighting till the King was dead.
They shake hands on it — all's peace —
as you were before the fighting started,
because the one in the middle said, 'You'd better.'
which is fine, but not for those between.
The freedom-fighters weren't to blame
for hitting what they didn't mean to.
The King's men weren't to blame being under orders
from the King to shoot the guerillas who were
potting them. Bad luck. And now
when the King says he will never never
shake hands with the guerilla again
and the freedom-fighter says never
till the King is shot dead,
who will be the smiler to say:
'Call it off, boys, till next time.'

The location for this set-up is
the cradle of faith, the birth-place of love.

II

You know how in the desert
there was nothing to eat for the chosen people
till it fell from God's sky,
white and momentary as snow —
a violation of nature, a disruption
of the organic personality of the desert
where death was its order. All very well

28

for the politician, one thing one day
another the next, that's diplomacy,
organization. He promises manna
which once consumed ceases to exist,
whereas the desert is rock, unconsolidated
but consistent to its own laws,
making credible the idea of finality,
and to disturb this was for God to
become a politician, for a moment the
creator less than the creation, nor
of it like the politician, who has
always a reason for doing that which
is palpably wrong to all, but him,
like arms for South Africa,
and at the same time he is a
Professor of the Christian Faith.
This is the nature of the politician.
He sloughs one skin at night and
puts on another in the morning.
These curious manipulations
are embarrassing to human observers,
but never to the Politician who
is protected from self-perception
and from observing the reactions
of human beings. There remains
the question — will it ever be possible
to bring together the human observer
and the Politician?

III
HIMMLER IS MY BROTHER

Once I took him for that
everything else followed naturally — the trains
trundling their loads to the gas chambers,
the station masters, guards, signal-men,
assistant signal-men at the points,
the villagers acknowledging the trains on their way,
accepting their processions as the final solution,
the trains singing to the rails:
'Himmler is my brother. Himmler is my brother.'

It is the solution of the desert,
of the mushroom that the Americans
first grew in the desert, of the
corrupting of the lungs, of the tree
that no longer breathes seed,
of the children of Vietnam
that no longer breathe
who ate of the tree of the
knowledge of evil. 'Himmler
is my brother, is my brother.'

In another country the sea lay on the right hand
and the clover flowered on the other.
The children ran after the small blue butterflies
that rose onto the air from the clover,
breathing its scent into their nostrils.
The mother called the children home
in the evening. In the morning the bell
called them to the village school.
Peewits flopped in the air.
Cows rubbed their hairy backs on posts.
In the school the children learned words
so that they could know of the desert far away
that would one day be their desert.

IV

'Sir,' I said, 'it is impossible,' and left.
The C O's instruction was to find three wells in
a thousand miles of Lybian desert.
He had it 'on authority,' he said,
'the Romans used them.' And in view of what
was going to happen when war broke out —
it was 1929 — it was essential to locate them;
'it might save the lives of British soldiers.'
I had a school friend posted near
El Alamein in charge of a camel corps.
He said: 'Yes, you can find the wells.
Go to the escarpment; get on a knoll;'
and he named it — the name was Egyptian
and doesn't stick with me — 'take your men
there and wait. In three weeks you'll know.'
So six men in turn, from a wooden tower

on top of a knoll from dawn to dark
watched the rim of the desert,
and no-one came. 'We'll stay for three
more days,' I said. On the second day
there was a smudge at the horizon.
It moved. They came — a dozen or so families,
men, women, children, camels, mules, goats,
hens, — and their gear. They were on their round.
It would end and begin again where they
had sown barley seed. They would cut
the plants that would be ready now with their
sickles, then sow more, then go on their way,
on their round, into the sun, over the sand
to another well to sow more. Their time was the height
of the sun and the length of their shadows;
the boundary of their country, the moving horizon.
When I could guess at their number
through glasses — sixty or so, not counting
the children, the huddle turned away, became
a snake, going east. I got into the transport,
an Austin Seven, and hared after them. They
stopped, when I came up to them in my cloud
of dust, as if under orders. Their faces
showed no interest. It was like being looked at
by a picture — the women behind their yashmaks,
all old faced, the men, scraggy, stripped of flesh,
with faces like scored cliffs, big feet
for the desert, large lean hands; the children,
black eyed, keeping the animals still,
one, his legs like sticks, tethered to a jackal
dog. There were infants, one being given suck.
Then the leader came, made in joints, to judge
by his walk, propelling himself with a bleached
staff, taller than himself. 'What did I want?'
They could not halt here. They must be
at the well by dark. He stood apart.
They watched him, silent. Round him,
round them, the desert. I watched them go,
diminish, move unhurried as if each movement,
every awkward jolt of the camels, whinny of mule,
lagging footstep of a child, had been pre-determined,
was repeating what had been done in this place,
this emptiness, a thousand times before.
At the horizon's bound I made for them,

came upon them gathering together.
The leader raised an arm high in gesture —
'Come.' It was the right time and place.
They gathered their whiteness about them
in the white blaze. Empty kettles and pots
clanked as the mules halted.
Eddies of sand stirred about their dirty
clothing as they rested. The sand
was a burning glass that threw the heat
back at their flesh and bones as they sat.
The boy with the dog went into himself;
waving date palms swung in his head,
bursting clouds sailed in his sky, waters
rushed between his green banks.
Then the camels sighed, men moaned
as they took themselves to their feet
for the way again, to leave behind
the smell of life that had gathered into
their circle, made it a habitation, a home,
a boundary of life, where life was insupportable.
'And there was nothing hid from the heat.'
I took bearings and noted on the map,
with protractor and compasses, the location.
I looked back to where they had made a place,
which was now again the desert. I looked forward
and could see no way.

Before night-fall they went through
the Breasts of the Virgin. Her stone chin
jutted above two sandstone rocks, moulded
by the wear of wind and sand, that narrowed
the way out of the round and so into a wadi
and down the dry bed — and beyond it to one side,
the well. They squatted, made fires; for
the first time children screamed, men shouted,
the dog barked, women gossiped, the camels
lowered themselves to the ground for unloading.
The water was fresh, not brackish. It was green
nearby, but little growth. No palms.
This water had watered the animals and people
of the Bedouins before the Romans came.
They had known the way to the well before Christ.
The well and the way to the well, the rocks
that would not move, and signs I could not see,

32

talked to the boy with the dog, imprinted a language
to carry the round of the course that was the year,
that was the measure of the desert, that was
his country, his home: and the language
would have travelled to his children and to
their children, but for what could not have been foreseen.

When Mussolini took over the Italian Empire
he asserted the boundaries on the map.
In the desert there are no boundaries,
only the shifting horizon. When the tribe
came to the Breasts of the Virgin,
they saw jack-boots that said:
'This is the boundary. Go back.'
They turned, knowing there was no
way back, no direction, no time that way,
— you cannot turn back time —
no return to a source, no water.
A British plane saw a straggle of
men, women, children, with animals —
and one behind on the desert.
The tribe died.

TRIBAL MAN

Whether it is shifty-eyed Smith
overlooking his blacks, Enoch Powell
innocently denouncing as God,
Nixon signing his for-ever treaties
with the Russians, throwing a loving
gesture to the Chinese with one eye,
the other on the next election, while
the peasant woman from the bombed
hospital in Hanoi drops in the ditch,
the dangerous tribe is man,
primitive as Paisley roaring
his non-Christian faith in Ireland,
or the gentle man Home, Sir Alec,
concluding another treaty to leave
things no worse than they are,
which is hell for the many,

or Breszhnev giving true democracy
to the Czechs, which means writing off
those who disagreed with his one-eyed
communism, nor did he forget
Solzhenitsyn.

10/6/72

THE LITTLE MATCH GIRL

There is
           a moment when
in our city Novembers
(this day) when

the river swings its spate against the
garden wall; debris plugs gutters, the mains
flood; just then
when an old man in a darkening room
looking through the transparent flesh held
against the flames — then

she stands amongst the brown leaves
in the back-garden, with the river bank
just beyond where the washing hangs,
pale with large eyes and straight thin hair
falling on her shoulders, aged
childhood into womanhood —

she is the little match girl.
One after another as dark falls
she lights her matches; they glimmer
momentarily, then drop silently
into the dark grass — one after
one after one after —

                    It is the regulation
scene of neglect, the condemnation
of the capitalists of the nineteenth century
who profited by starving the people
who worked for them, then charitably

34

starting Christmas charities. Those poor
died so that the Great British Empire and the Good
Queen could show the World how Great was Britain.

We do it differently.
In the last match she is aflame.
She burns at my back-door in Vietnam
or wherever.

POLITICS

I
For a time it was
'Gentlemen.'
Later
'Friends.'
Then after the change of regime
'Comrades.'

In any case the processed
applause — 'Small crowd applauding'
Disk 75289X — was the same for each.

II
In Florence
they have a nice economy.
On Saint Antony's day they display
banners for the saint. The next
day being the first of May
the reverse side is shown —
Hammer and Sickle.

III
In Ireland they do it differently,
Fratricide.

THEOLOGICAL PIECES

I
I dig the garden for a worm
for a hook.
'Uncle,' said the worm to me,
'Do not put me on the hook
or I shall remind you ever after
that you have been on one
since they kicked you out of Eden.'

II
The coal mine of my mind
is sufferable
when others acknowledge the condition
as theirs; less so when officials
of the mysteries
insist they have a searchlight.

III
'O.K.' said the Master of the Mysteries,
'but who is going to shed light, if I don't.
Try an expert in defoliation —
a geneticist.'

'One day,' said the geneticist,
'I shall come up with a man who
will see through the coal face
and round the world
till he gets a back view of himself.'

IV
My face is a cliff face
scarred.
A hole in the middle opens.
'God.'

I eat another apple.

WORM

I
Earth movers who
move it by
passing it through their strip,
leaving it at their other end,
their ten hearts beating as one.

This action
predetermined the rose
that still sheds blood
on this December day.

II
The adoration of the rose
is the adoration of the worm.
Praise Freud
who gave another Eden.

III
Love still is
when two are one.
This I know
for so
I was begun.

IV
No serpent.
No Eden.

ANGELS' WINGS OR WHATEVER

When I was very young, a sprightly angular boy,
they were everywhere, but especially under my feet,
lifting me up — I went loping through the air,
(as all the Stars, football and female, do now)
in slow motion — so I was captain of the football team.
They called me to the rooftops and I climbed
in the dizzy air. It whisked around my big ears,
my nostrils gathered the sea-smell from far-away waters;
my eyes collected the bright beach and the rocking boats
in the little harbour at one go. I sat on the golden roof top.

       'What is the laddie daein there?
       Why does he no come doon?'
        'I'd gie him a skelp on the bare
       backside gin he'd been my loon.'

And not a wing in sight. I'm old. They're back.
Black winged and bloody mouthed they buzz finance.
The blind business man takes them for fruit,
the generals for friendly war-heads,
the scientist developments of the genetic code,
the New Left for the resurrection of Karl Marx,
the New Right for an English Christ to destroy black power.
Would God the skies were empty again!

MORALITIES

Used to steal turnips,
swedes, with blue tops,
long light-green shaws.
This was allowed.

Once — they grew in open fields —
greenpeas, two thin boys
with arse-holed shorts,
stole. Immoral.

ANGELS

For fear they were not there I
could not look at the spring-green trees.
For fear they were not hanging
from the catkinned branches
I looked away.

I said to myself:
'All this unexplained energy,
all these hanging delicacies
and the slow vegetable trunk,
isn't than enough?
You don't need angels.'

Now they hurl themselves
about the sky,
shout doom.
I can't look up for fear.

FOLK

SINGLE TICKET — EDINBURGH/BENNACHIE

'I made up ma face to gang oot
but I made up my mind to stay in,'
she said. Help! Page a psychiatrist,
or a poet or a fiction writer or an architect,
or a Scottish stock-broker. 'Well hen,' says
the stock-broker, 'what ye need is an entrepreneur.
He can go between, and I'm the very boy for that.'
A passing Professor of Linguistics remarked
there was a distinction to be made between
the use of 'made up' with respect to the face
and the mind. The fiction writer said:
'Who done it? It's a whodunit. Who made up
her mind? Who was in the house at the time?
It had green shutters and there was a father.'
The mathematician said it was an 'unresolved equation.'
The architect said: 'It is a question of room space.'
The poet said nothing. The lecturer in linguistics
returned to say the problem was linguistic.
Was she Scottish? Was she English? She was
the split product of a split nation.
'Mass schizophrenia,' said the psychiatrist,
'incurable, terminal.' ('The Scottish antisyzygy'
murmured the poet, but nobody heard.) 'And
there is no dialogue between the personae!'
'An fa's speakin,' says Ma breengin in
fae ooter space jist as the conversash
is gettin hetted up. 'Naebody's speakin
tae naebody. An neen o' ye is gyan tae hae onything
tae dee with my dochter. She's comin stracht back
tae the back o' Bennachie, wi her Ma, faur there's
nae personality nor linguistic problems,
faur Natur rins the burnie tae the sea
wi'oot let or hindrance, faur naebody
maks up their faces, an aabody's
made up their minds lang syne.'

AN INTERVIEW WITH REMBRANDT

It was, of course, an impertinence to expect
even an admission. He was, as we believed,
in the Seventh Heaven. Some said he had
Identified with God, but that was putting it
a bit high. He was not to be seen, but
might be heard if he cared to utter.
Decidedly he would respond to a question.
'Rembrandt Harmenszoon van Rijn', I said,
(the informality of the Christian name only
was out of the question in heaven.) 'it is
your immense charity that shines from
the faces of the people you honoured in paint.
What was your inspiration?' A voice said:
'They peyed me for't, but nae weel eneuch.
Hardly the cost o the paint an canvas.'
'But' said I — we were off course — 'all
these years these images on the walls
have spoken of humanity. Saskia — '
'Saskia' the voice muttered, 'Ah Saskia!'
'And the woman in bed pushing back the curtain.'
'Her? Weel, there was a spare bit canvas.
She was a dacent body — dacent to me.
An the licht was on her. Licht'
he said, 'let there be licht.'

There was a pause. I could hear heavy breathing.
I thought he might have been a little more revealing.

REMBRANDT IN AGE
Self-portrait in the National Gallery of Scotland

He kent, as thae een lookt at his
oot o the dark he made in yon picter,
he lookt on a man, himsel, as on
a stane dish, or leaf faa'in in winter,
that calm was his strang souch.
But in that dark twa wee lichts,
een that shone like lit windaes,
an in that hoose muckle business,
words an kindnesses atween folk.
Aa that steir in Rembrandt's heid,
or, as some wud say, in's verra saul.

WOMAN PITTEN BACK NICHT
'A Woman in Bed' by Rembrandt (National Gallery of Scotland)

Risin on ae elbuck frae the box bed
wi rumpelt claes on't, she lifts,
on the back o' her foreairm, the fall
an lets the licht luik in, syne stops
so's to catch up wi a new day.
He sees her, thinkin, 'Wife — nae bonny,
but sonsy, strang,' syne luiks again,
an what he sees he pits in paint.

Noo a'body gangin by yon woman
in the picter maun stop an luik again,
for yon was first-licht he saw
on her brow. He made her
as love traivelt thru's ee til's haun
an intae thae merks on a bit canvas.

45

THE NICHTWATCH

'The Nightwatch' by Rembrandt
(Rijksmuseum, Amsterdam)

Dab hauns at the money gem, he thocht.
'Mind the step, Maister, as ye gang ben.'
They cam in tae get pentit, bleat wi pride,
padded burghers — ('burghers' did ye say?
Weel, let it staun at that the whiles.')
Rembrandt gets on wi the wark. Ootside
they're for hame, ilk ane dressed
tae the nines, siller buckles on their shuin,
ruffs whiter than a swan's down feathers.
An say they felt — as pure as snaw,
til hame, an bed, sarks aff, breeks aff.
They weemen's nae doot the stuff they're o'.
They haud their gab forbye, but Rembrandt kens.
Ilk ane for what he was, he kens, nae foozlin
him, but he kent tae they micht be waur,
as weel as better. Sae he pentit them,
nae naukit tae the bane — was he no a man
himsel — nae starkers, but *sympatico*,
but nae eneuch tae please his maisters.
Ŋa, na, this was 'letting the side down.
It wasn't cricket. Wasn't the man being paid
good rates for the job.'

This day three hunder year
sin syne, or mair, they glower, or peek, or luik
oot o' their dark, or raither Rembrandt's dark,
wi licht i' their ee. Was that no eneuch
to be alive as that, while we lie doon
nicht by nicht in oor benichted sauls:
nae sun, nae stars abune, nor mune,
encapsulate in concrete, or airn, or
God keens whit, waitin for the nameless
finish.

Would that Rembrandt or God would luik
wi seein ee intil oor ee that yet can tak
an gie a little licht — the Licht itsel, mebbe.

46

A HIND'S DAUGHTER
by Sir James Guthrie
(National Gallery of Scotland)

Nae kailyard here! Nae clarty dubs.
Nae feeling looks, nae heivenly thochts abune,
Nae gentlin a'athing owre wi saps.
Nae dribblin at the chaps and doffin caps
Or gien a nod tae God to say, 'It's me.'
But here cabbages sproot.
A quine wi a sharp blade in her haun
stauns in a field at Cockburnspath
richt as she did.

THE VEGETABLE STALL
by W Y Macgregor (National Gallery of Scotland)

'Stall?' Na, 'sta' — a wuiden bench wi a wa ahint. For Sale —
tatties, neeps, ingans, leeks, carrots, kail, rhubarb —
the hail jing-bang o' needfu products o' yirth, in paint
as doon-richt as a Clyde boat-builder's haimmer, an that's
whaur Macgregor belanged. He says tae his freens and learners:
'Hack the subject oot, as you were usin an aix.'
Kokoshka cam by, lookit lang an lang at Macgregor's picter.
Hardly possible, he thocht and said: 'To think this picter
was made afore I was born.' In auchteen-eighty fower
Macgregor brocht thae objects and paint thegither,
louped the gap, ilk stroke to mak tatties, neeps, rhubarb,
themsels in truth, that's new an auld, on that canvas
that stares at his, aye yet, this day, as time stude still
frae then till noo. O tae hae sic sicht thru hand an brain
tae stop the universe in'ts track, an see't for what it is!

47

CHOPIN AT 10 WARRISTON CRESCENT — 1848
for Alicja Danuta Fiderkiewcz — pianist — 1974

I
Thunder and silver — the air trembling.

We came upstairs with the invalid Chopin
climbing the turning stairs, Everest without oxygen,
then taking all his heartache into his music,
blood on the stones of Warsaw, memories
of his defiant country and its terrible history,
he put them down, inarticulate marks on a white sheet.

You, a girl, found his heart in your fingers.
The red deepens in the roses,
the dark rages outside the panes.
The refugees are taking to the roads, old guns fire;
despair rattled the bones of the frail man
at the piano, who was about you in that room.
'Remember,' he said, 'not a dying man — '
Dry leaves dance in the street,
in the salons mazurkas and polonaises,
the banners of liberty on the snow, scatter,
are taken into the future in a small room
in another country.

II
It wis the cold that got ye,
and yon twisty stairs; you sclimmin
them like yer hert tae burst,
Everest wi-oot oxygen tae you —
syne at the tap, the piano
an ootside leaves gan heilster-gowdie.
Ye were fair connach'd,
or sae we thocht, but some pooch
in yer hert had virr that ettled
tae win oot, an did, in your fingers
till thon hoose rocked in your thunner.
The siller leddies, hauns in their laps,
gied naething awa; the gents
lookt like stookies (an mebbe were)

48

but you soon't oot a' rooms an ha's
an ower a' watters tae Europe
an across the plains wi snaw
whaur merched the Poles, an
puir folk wi a' their warldly gear
upon the roads — thae refugees,
then an noo.
                    An so's your music
then an noo in a lassie's fingers,
makin sic steir, the air tremmlin,
speakin your leid, your folk's leid,
an oors, a' wha bide haudin
tae themselves, that benmaist thing
that dwalls, waitin for the kinlin
till the spark loups at the hert.
Then a' the trash o' the warld's
forgot, a' the riff-raff wi naethin
i their heids but the neist kick
o' the ba that lang syne's burst.

'Tak hert' says your sang. The snaw
tummles on Scotland and you're awa.
'Maks nae odds. I'm in that sang
that soon't yestreen, the-day,
an will dae the-morn an a'.'

AE NICHT FIRE-BLEEZE

In Memoriam Barbara Hepworth (1903-1976)
who died in a fire in her home in Cornwall

Night. Nicht. Wha's?
The nicht was hers, her

that strung strings athwart the rock
tae mak dumb mass gie sang.
Then, thonder, ae nicht fire-bleeze,
a lowe on the warld's rim, a sun
that ate the doors o' the wast
ridin the watters, takin
till its end humanity.

Them that kens that kens a'.
Was't no eneuch tae sign her mortality
in veins ridin the skin, blear een,
crevasses dug in her broo, an wyte,
gien her ae last chance tae gawk
at winter tree an mak it bleeze
wi Spring in'ts form, her takin't
frae Natur tae gie it tae oor natur,
so's when we lookt the flooers lookt
oot anew. She took stane o' a' kind,
marble — black, gree, Parian, white
alabaster, ironstane, pink Ancaster
stane; the wuids — red-wuid, rose-wuid,
sycamore, African black-wuid, beech-wuid
an a' ither tae uncover in theirselves
purity in essence. But she's nae here tae
tell the tale in daith is life, in lumpen licht.

But noo I look on the Burnet rose,
a composition in white marble,
ilk petal a marvel o' precision.
Touch — ilkane as saft as flesh,
an scentit sweet an shairp.
The flooers float in air,
the roots trail in aneath the rock,
traivellin the bank tae get a haud
o' yon yird that's Scotland,

50

tae souk watter an iron mell't
thegither, an synes travaig
the sap o' life alang thae veins
till oot intae the peelie-wallie sun
that we've brewed up in Scotland
tae mak dee for the real thing.

Noo, when she in Cornwall
coost the clean shape o' things
in truth, was't no for his tae,
for aabody, as when yon rose
gies sheen tae oor pit-mirk,
that tae's for her an his an a'.

300 DAYS RAIN

I stood at the window
and watched it dripping down,
dropping down the window pane.
Across the street — the School.
Holidays — hurrah! And the rain rained
on the school and on the grey street.
Said to my Dad: 'How long?'
'Wind's in the East.' He said,
'Three days at least.' Three
hundred days I stood. Stood.
And the school was not washed away.
And the boats did not sail in the street.
And our headmaster was not drowned.
And there was no call for Noah.
There was nothing. 'Nowt' but drops
dropping on the pane till one o'clock,
when Doughy, the big man with the big
moustache at the burroo who paid
the workless workers their dough,
came swinging up the street, swinging
his rolled umbrella up the street
and singing! Swaying full sail
to our sharp-right corner. Would he
bloody his bald head with the
black bowler hat on the black
railings as, half-seas over, he
swung out? 'He'll do it,' said
my Dad. 'Shorten sail!
Hold hard! List to port!'
Like a feather in a gale,
true as a glass of whisky
he rounds the point — and gone.
And gone my bliss, and the three
hundred days of my seventh birthday
go on and on and on . . .

AT H C ANDERSON'S HUS — ODENSE
for Kai Greiber

So, before the little mermaid swam
into him, before the little match girl
and the vain emperor, before the snow queen
and the constant tin soldier, the nightingale,
and the dog with eyes as large as tea-cups,
the dream that dreamed up the painted houses,
red-coated postmen, top-hatted chimney sweeps,
cobbled streets, yellow lamps and the dark,
the fairy tale was written into the stones
that waited for the poor boy to grow
to tell the tales that knocked on doors
at nights like drums that drummed, 'All's well!'

KAREN, AGE 1

She knows
the flower in the grass
beckons her.

It does not move.
Its yellow eye
looks straight to heaven.

She stares
at the day's eye,
would pick it up.

Towering, toppling,
her body equivocates,
wavering

till it stands erect again
still swaying as if
straining in a great wind.

Then flops on her bottom
on the green grass.
Daisy stares to heaven.

She ponders her long day.
The earth presents its fruit
to her immense grasp.

A dog barks far off
in his other world.

CHILD AND TREE IN AUTUMN

Last night's rains ran the river mute
giving no sound to the morning's sun.
The fir plantation bends to the flowing hill
down which a straggle of copper beeches take
their doused fires to the water's edge.
From the bank the haws' red suns flare;
drenched rowans shake their fruits above.
Herds with swaying udders fulfil
the autumn day. Painted by a child
a house sits square in the middle.
Upstairs a face at a small pane peeks,
travels the canvas as if it might tear open,
the precarious moment swallowed in dark.

GOOD MORNING

Feet squelch on a brown Monday morning
that hasn't had time to put its face on.
Gutters run. A bus washes the corner with mud.
A child, nose flattened against the glass,
sees the world new. In his heaving ship
churned-up slush is a wake of creaming waves.
A woman in a green hat, stuttering on high heels,
is Spring. I am in his looking glass and hear
hooves' thump of lambs' dance on thin turf.

It pushes them up into the blowing sky.
As the boat moves out smooth beyond the cliff head
my long drowned innocence rises and breathes again.
Those aboard have no truck with water,
that has killed their generations, but to hunt fish.
It is nothing but a use that will exercise cruelty
as wanton as malformation. 'Good morning!'
Is this then a lie that the absurd face at the pane
conveys, seeing miracles where there are none,
but that the eyes are wonders.

LAMENT FOR THE PASSING OF THE HISSING OF THE STEAM TRAINS

for Jennifer

Now the grandfathers tell
their grandchildren,
'There was no thing like the hiss
of a steam train.

Wisps of white
swam over wheatfields,
encircled briar roses,
fled into the blue,
went boldly over Russian snows.
When they cut down the Cherry Orchard
steam trains were heard.

Now that steam trains are gone
we should give up hissing
for joy
as do the ripe cornfields
as we passed in summer winds,
as does the bell heather in light
air trembling as we passed by the glen,
as do the soft small waves
on the shingle beach under a quiet moon.'

Never, never, never, never,
will they see, hear the great
gonged trains go so again.

LOST BOY — LIVERPOOL STREET STATION 1918

The legs bandaged in khaki, big boots
clobbering the ground. Bound trunks
of limbs going up into suffocating nothing.
Escape. The hand of the father held my fist
tight, till suddenly it rose away on important
business. Cigar. I smelt it. An unseen thread
pulled me through the labyrinth, and I was there
at *The Rocket*, at the gleaming brass body,
the bright tall chimney pointing skyward.
'Please put a penny in *The Rocket*.'
Wheels go round. Some day it will move
out of its glass prison, will chortle
and steam, throwing up white plume.

Through a sweet countryside wisps of white
swam over wheatfields. My steam train
picked its way through strawberry patches,
heading hard for our cold north suns,
entered dark glens, trembling the bell heather,
shouted a little as the sea hove in sight,
ran by it as the small waves beat their own
time on the shingle beaches under the full moon
that had filled our mouths with silver
bellied herring for as long as my black-bearded
grandfather had roared: 'Praise the Lord!'
to welcome the boats to port. 'Toot', said the Lord
as we slid between the sea and clover to the stone
platform grunting and grinding, pshawing to a halt.
Our white plume rose on its column and spread — home.

'You were lost, you understand, lost.' Lost?
Why shake me so? I did not kick, bite, scream.
Better that we do. The boy dreams.
We have our nightmares.

OLD MAN AND CHILD
seen through a window pane

Bone of my bone, old bones,
rags and bones you are: through
frosted glass under a yellowed
sun he stoops to a yellow crocus,
will do so till earth slips from him,
and he marooned on the island of self.

Dance boy, dance on the bright grass.
It throws you high to the sun.
Dance, dance, you are light to my day.
You throw no shadow over my way.

LEAF FALLS FOR OLD MAN

Holding his eyes to the hardening
earth, the inconsequential moment
becoming dust as it fell from blue,
scarlet and sere, the leaf, rocking,
turning a slow spiral in the still air,
its veins dull red riding the skin,
he witnessed his joy becoming him.

This fall persuades there is no sere,
no flint, but calls to winter bird
and beast and and man to bed soft down.

NORTH COAST CHERRIES
for Elizabeth

All around
salt in the wind
a mile from the sea
salt on the tongue.

Against the wall
that faced south
sweet red cherries
enjoyed by stealing boys.

When I think of you
through many winters
cherries ripen
in the sun.

JANUARY HAIKU
for Elizabeth

She sits in
Arizona sun
snow on low
juniper and dry grass.

Do not disturb
this moment. Wind
blows, dust rises.
Time takes away space.

Sit still in this
moment elected
by who knows what.
Now dew beads grass.

SONNET ON MY WIFE'S BIRTHDAY

All the love I have will not take her years away:
All the knowledge given not grant her time release,
Yet one day less impoverishes this great feast
That grew when we together went our way,
Hurrying to meet our newly planted day,
That barely showed above the stony ground
Of our North-East, whose grudging air beat down
The rare freedom that becomes when two are one.
So, when every loss is gain, as every colour, brown
Or red or tarnished yellow in our life's spectrum,
Shows itself, why should we protest too much
Against the silent pace that makes in us such
Speed, for we have learned to plant our love so strong
Our children's children now take up the song.

OLD SNAPSHOT

The camera's shutter clicked. He'd caught
her for himself alone, he thought,
standing slim among the marguerites
against a sunny, summer wall with apples
on it. He put her in his pocket book in 1932.

The sepia mellows, seems to tell more true,
not just that moment long ago; collects
the happiness that walked through shady lanes
and by St Machar's towers at crook of Don
and through the Auld Toun's clattering streets,
by-passing the Bishop founder's tomb, to King's,
to sit amongst old words long dried on the page,
mountains of them, beautiful and boring,
wise and absurd — and still the moment breathes,
disturbs their dust.
                    Another place, another time,
from which she still looks out from that mute world
amongst the flowers, grown now most delicate.

59

And all the air of this dull day is changed.
Landscapes shout new with Spring. Seas glitter
in their calm, and I, this breathing animal,
own such sweet strangeness as no words will do.

ELIZABETH POLISHING AN AGATE

My love, you are pulled into a stone.
The skies run into night,
The stone stars are there.
In this lost momentary world
you treasure stone under your hand,
seek out what is most unlike,
smoothing stone like glass
till its fixed hair lines,
finer than Leonardo's line,
mirror stone's permanence.
There are no seasons in a stone.
Lode star it draws you,
you giving your brief warmth
to stone.
Gone, it stays cold.

PERSPECTIVES

ABORIGINE WITH TAX FORM

' . . . even though you are reared in a city out there, you're
liable to feel when the hot wind blows, that the city would,
in fact, be blown away and that you would be faced with
this kind of interminable, extraordinary bush landscape which
goes on for ever.'

Sydney Nolan

He was in the taxation office in Sydney,
(God knows why) — and with a tax form,
a white paper (A4) with words printed
on it and question marks. He was
one brown, gnarled, grizzled, almighty
question mark under the electric light
of the concrete edifice: his category —
'black' he insisted. Place of residence —
'Australia.' Home — 'Australia.' Still
nothing on paper, his fist on the page.
Outside, the hard sun was on his fellows.
They sat on their hunkers on the flat
stone paving. Tower-blocks soared skywards.
Steel, glass, the synthetic scape took over.
Not quite; in Sydney the sea is not to be
denied. Sun beams its flash into high-rise
executive suites: it gets a peek at the stock-exchange:
it interrupts art lovers in the gallery of N S W.
Insurance blocks in George Street are the less secure
for its glance. Its smell settles on roof-top
restaurants. Seagulls thieve food at the Opera House.
Budgies flutter their colours. Pelicans, even,
float around in city airs. Sea, air-borne dwellers,
disturb the city abstract, ask questions
that will not stay in the parameters of paper.
Inside H Q taxation, Sydney, they play taped
soft western country muzak to assuage Australian
tax-payers' nerves. Inside he is still there.
Head down, the crumpled features, visible just,
the broad nostrils, till an upward glance,
flickering eyelids betray brown eyes —
staring at the black marker on white paper —
see nothing. For him nothing is there.

He is become a no-person, an astronaut
who has lost touch with his ship,
becoming vibrations on a scanner,
will be so until he puts foot on earth,
his earth which grew this dark earth man,
who named Australia's birds as they cried:
kookaburra, kookaburra raucous, currawong,
currawong — a song, a morning song in flight,
wurra-wurra, cooee-coee — koel calls,
bock-bock-oo, bock-bock-oo gobbles wompoo
pigeon, oom-oom-oom woops pigeon, jabiru
— silent hunter, brolga — trumpets brolga:
ear echoes to calls' bounds and re-bounds off
cliff-face, rocks, silver-barked trees,
waters boom, sky will black with thunder.
The red fire-god raves through the brush:
all is ultimate, so this man-Adam lights his
home places alive with sounds — Andamooka,
Thunda, Goorajoo, Nooka Warra, Croajingalong,
Wagga Wagga, Woolanmarroo, Booroorban, Boort,
Boonoo Boonoo, Murrumbidgee, Murrburrah. 'Ha!'
But *he* calls out for the newborn world.
He calls out with the astonishment of the child.
'Oo!' 'Aa!' cries the child as the stars were
new made for her, for him, for the whole being
child is. 'Kangaroo!' shouts child in man,
and the original is made. It thumps, pounds,
leaps, is at one with no man's land.
'Warringin' — wild dog, the teeth are bared
in the word: dried grit, sharp stone in the word,
and the land stretches its bone in an eternity
of distance: no living land, but suns, dawn to dark,
will not blaze away the guana still as rock
at its rock. From Dream Time, (altjira bugari),
the founding drama of sky and earth, the beings
of the kingdom, all creatures — man being one — came.
From then a spiny ant-eater, with sensing snout,
moves out from stone to seek its food, survives
as *he* survives in this, the land he shares with gods
— the animals, so he acknowledges them the inheritors
of that first great stroke. They honoured him
by their presence — all in the rite of life, the dance
and song of life. The water in the water-hole
is the water of life for all life. Here in drought

the animals drink their fill, and no spear
will pierce their hides. This is the Secret Place,
forbid to hunter, place of mystery, of renewal
of flesh and spirit life, of being. Bird, beast
and the desert tree whose root drives down as deep
as branch's tip points skywards, draw from the source
of life-song. The bond between all kind stayed desert,
till the white man came with his guns
and Jesus. Jesus, black Jesus, was in the eyes
of the children. The white man did not see Jesus
in the eyes of the children. He saw black savages
who blocked the way of progress. In the name of progress
and Christian civilisation they increased productivity.
The commodity, sugar was in demand. They imported
Kanakas blacks from the Solomons, efficient hands.
The Kanakas yearned for their home ways and meat.
On Sundays the white men went to church.
After church they gave guns to their workers,
who killed for meat the people of the land,
who when they stood, stood as tall cedars,
when they moved were clouds walking,
when they ran it was as the antelopes,
every syllable of their being uttering
the messages from the generations back,
in the movements of legs and arms,
the gestures of hands and fingers,
the planting of feet on the ground,
the rhythm of torso and thighs and breathing.
Christ wept in the eyes of the children.
In Sydney in the taxation office, the official,
pale, slim lady in a grey suit with handkerchief
peeping in a red pyramid from her breast pocket,
looked kindly on the native. 'The Aranda tribe,
I think?' she said: yes, but in Aranda speech
there is no word for tribe. The bond is speech.
The Katitja, Iliaura, Unmattiera, are bound
in intimacy and ritual by Aranda speech.
Now he is seeing his journeys, the sand, spinifex —
roots, grubs, lizards for food: the long walk
in the night air, in daytime sand and rock burn.

Day dawns: it is home: crickets chirp insistent
from river grass: birds shout: streams talk:
voices echo from the gum trees' shiny bark:

he is made anew. Brothers, sisters, mother,
father would welcome him — but no-one. None.
Kangaroo and emu fall to the white man's gun.
Sweet meadow grass turns to dust. Where was song
a new desert. 'You need assistance,' she said.
'An aroma of animal and earth,' she felt,
'hung about the office after he had gone.'
She saw them in a huddle shambling on the street.
They smiled, giggled, their shoulders shook:
laughter, outrageous as a kookaburra, explodes.

ASTRONOMER

Now going into the presumed ends of the universe
he listens to the faint illiterate stars.
He has placed his warm heart on stone faces
he does not know, in undefined wildernesses
wandering to chart what has happened
beyond belief aeons ago.

He is a number to a number to
a computer to a number.
He is an equation waiting
for an equation, an equation
which is Astronomer.

In the interstices of time and space
a sparrow fell. Teach us,
the bleak discoverers how
to witness to time and space
and to the blood of a sparrow.

IS JAMES? IS JANEY THERE?

Why do they do it to us — these phone voices,
thinned down like Giacometti sculptures
to next to nothing? 'Is Jamie there?'
it seems to say — plaintive, female — and I,
'No. Who?' Is Janey there or was it someone
else? Who speaks. She won't tell. Why not?
Exist — does she? Conned. I am connected with
space only. I am a chance component in an
electronic module formulated to utter: 'Is
James, is Janey there?' Where? Not here — where?
Who? Is there a candidate for being, a something
that may become the instant another says — 'Yes.'
'No!' I deny existence to the given. Given:
James, Jamie, Janey — electronically composed.
Answer the question on one side of the page.
Translate into persons. The question presupposes
an examinee. This machine is a word-maker.
James, Jamie, Janey do not materialize.
Sad toned they swim in their universe
like astronauts, who have lost touch
with their ship, who have become vibrations
on a scanner, will be so, till he put
a foot on earth. 'City of the dead'
said Scott at Pompeii. But they had walked
with friends, lit fires, embraced at night,
talked face to face to become themselves.

THE PSYCHIATRIST TO HIS LOVE

(Experiments at Edinburgh University have
shown that if a person is deprived of dreams at
night, hallucinations will follow during the day)

'Ah, my sweet,' said the psychiatrist
to his love, 'now that I can
deprive you of your dreams at night,
you will have them open-eyed in the day-time.'

He took the sweet smelling pines
that stood by her white sea,
the leopard, the lamb and the serpent,
and the white ass from her dream, the
lily cloud that sheltered him from the
sun in her night, the moon-lit beaches
where she walked in her advertisement,
the furbelows and flounces,
the mutton-chop sleeves and the
embroidered petticoat from her sleep
and put them in the box for morning.

During the day he gave them all
back to her. 'Sour milk,' she said,
a wounded old woman. 'Put them back
into the dark,' she said.

MAN IS NOT A FISH
for Mark Horner, swimmer

He is a fish as the water falls from him
as he encloses himself in that fluent glass
to be nothing but one things as starry suns
fly to his lips in the lapping water.
In the faint green, angel fish flit,
transparencies: an absurd crab scuttles
on the floor: no world for speculators,
but being. This is not the element

68

for the forked mammal imitative
of fish perfection, weighted by his thinking
machine.
What god is propitiated as the body
in a bow-bend stretches in a split second, striking
the hard film, yet being received softly into a depth.

All our knowledge is nothing before that incoherence.
All our words burst as bubbles at a surface.

THE RUNNER

This race I run alone.
Hands dangling, limbs loose, waiting
the moment of entry eye catches eye
of daisy left of dirt track on a green plain.
I run. I lift the green grass into myself.
Breathing lengthens and pulls with
calf muscles, thigh muscles. Change
stride: go lope for distance. Strain.
The drummer heart demurs. Slacken.
I find self in the iris of the daisy,
contained by white petals in the calyx vest.
Now it carries mind. What was
ground rooted now a yellow sun
to be held, to hold mind's eye.
Wings beat in the brain, I stay,
take earth into sky. Into the
meadows of my poverty the sun
steps. I am earth and light.
Clouds move under my feet.

SING

Written for my students in wheel
chairs at a poetry class, St Andrews
College, North Carolina

Curious that
in our circumstances
amongst the hurt
we sing.

To sing we tear
the veil of reason
to make a vessel
for love.

See, it spills over
nor shall any catch
such drops who will not
know the blind god.

POETRY CIRCLE IN A SQUARE ROOM

In the centre of the room
a squat man in a bulgy suit
has put his cap under the chair
upside down into which he coils
a snake like a scarf.
He knows it is not a snake.

It might be convenient it it were
for his nostrils sense the
woman enter, seat herself behind
in the far corner. As she crosses
her legs under the red silk
dressing gown there is the
silk worm sound in his ear.

She contemplates the grey,
horn-rimmed girl with the flat
shoes (perhaps she can write)
sitting on the outermost edge,
angular in the front row.
She opens a new note-book.

Snow falls. Snow falls.
A black cat is at the window.
The lecturer will not let
the poem in, dismisses
its green eyes to the darkness.
The black cat leaps from the snow,
stares at the pane,
silent, asserting nothing:
leap — a felt movement,

effortlessly creating the
moment that is one thing,
her poise, less precarious,
she acknowledges, perhaps,
our world inside. The snow,
a blank page, acknowledges
her delicate tread, her imprint
of a moon-lit traverse.

Precise shadow, you are
a presence to be shut out.
Admitted, your intolerable
completeness would destroy us.

WINTER MATTER

We have visitors who would prefer
not to be known, squeaking and prattling
along corridors. I leave a little
provender for them — cheese.
No traps, no such unkindness.

These are country people seeking
the warmth of our home, have come
into the city homeless refugees
from blasted fields, wrecked
by secret agents. At night

I come downstairs, barefoot,
a cold foot on linoleum. One
is there, or is it another,
less welcome. Big brother is
throwing his boozy weight about.

The house shudders. These are not
the eyes that bead gently in the gloom.
These bite the hand that feeds,
lodgers, who come to kill, eat flesh.
Wood rots, stone cracks, fire eats.

That's the way it is these days.
Everything gets out of hand.
No place for decency.

JANUARY VISITORS

We were visited by bullfinches
this Monday morning. Immediately
we were in an exclusion zone: barriers
were set up: the chemical destructs
we had absorbed from laden airs
flotated from us: the neuroses,
the nagging knowledge that our governors
were insane power seekers, the desperations,
vanished. Subtly these formal presences —
neat fitted black caps, deep-pink down chests —
persuaded us into their limbo.
Each green blade that pushed through snow,
each crumb set on the stone window sill,
presented itself in that new light of day.
(Yet through the pane the shadowed human face
that could not know that other place
where no time is, but every moment now.)

72

They sang no songs.
Doubtless they had no concern for us.
Doubtless they came for a meal.
Doubtless it was fortuitous they chose
our backyard for their landfall,
for that momentary enlightenment: gone
in a flirt of wings.

GITANJALI

**On being asked for
a poem 'for India'**

Outside my window
leaves from the sycamore
blow about my patch.
Over the low stone wall
a muddied path, a tangle
of tussock grass, weeds,
the Water of Leith,
no holy river Ganges,
no Lethe, a mud brown,
swollen burn charging
in spate, bearing away
one thigh boot, two oil drums,
one arm-chair — the stuffing
milked by the water, a stained
white cloth unwinding slowly —
city detritus heading fast
for the Forth and the North Sea.
My stare telescopes on the brown,
but who is this large-eyed,
black-haired girl — child,
brown as of the water,
in a long robe to thin ankles,
suddenly grown in my garden?
She stands in the welter.
Her grave eyes look at me,
Motionless she holds a ball.
It has landed on my plot.
I smile at her. 'It is not

important,' but she
stands silent. She looks
upon the ball as if she
held in her hand her world
of pain and laughter.
She is from India.
'Your name?' I ask.
She does not answer, does not
look from the silvered ball,
bright with intermingled colours
flowing, unending in the round.
Slowly she lifts her eyes to mine.
'Gitanjali.' I do not catch the word.
'Gitanjali,' her name. 'Song Offering.'

Gitanjali was the name of Tagore's first published book
of poems, which name was given to the Indian poet who
died in her seventeenth year.

CHILDREN'S CHRISTMAS PARTY

In the white room into which I glance,
as the afternoon fades its brown,
a tree has grown shining with silver.
A boy sucking a lollipop rides a horse.

Two girls make a cat's cradle with string.
A fat boy eats. The little girl
in the red dress with blue ribbons
in her hair opens her big eyes wide

to acclaim the admiration of mothers.
Suddenly they are all in a ring
about the tree. They throw up their white
arms waving. They sing soundless songs

to silent music for the dance.
What is all this worship? This wonder?
in which they walk and utter,
that spreads like magic

74

about the trees that become strange
as they are strangers to him deafened
by thin glass. Outside as soft rain falls,
as unseeing her round mouth laughs

into the night, I am for a moment
in them, it seems, but they are stars apart.

AT THE VILLA DEI MISTERI, POMPEII

The sacred Agape! A young girl bears a dish
with votive ornaments. Silenus plays his lyre.
A dancing satyr gapes. The Bacchante kneels,
touching a drape that conceals the object:
of love, fecundity and peace. Another
in formal dance, dances in exultation.
Prelude to the act the bride initiate
waits upon the mystery of the ceremony.
Dionysus, god of generation and the dead,
communicator of the loving cup, she waits
the phallus unveiled; her bowed flesh
accepts the whip. Now she stands poised
on this two thousand year old wall
that did not crumble when Vesuvius roared,
where still the lustration of the fire glows
from red walls about the dancers that shed
their pallid light.
                    A party of German tourists
take over the room, packed, back to back,
face to face, backs to walls. Their guide
recites the facts, the facts, the facts.
Knowledge and incomprehension spread;
a rash on bland faces. 'Tomorrow Athens!'

O goddess Athene! O Neptune, Poseidon, Venus, Aphrodite!
Diana — presider over glittering oceans. O Mediterraneo!

ODD GOINGS-ON IN DUNFERMLINE TOUN

In yon gusty toun on the slope, folk
slip aff it, disappear,
gang in an oot o' doors
fast, like in auld films,
uphill thin man roon corner,
doonhill fat man intae shop,
lassies intae trees,
auld men intae ruins,
rinnin boys intae the grun,
auld wife gangs heilster gowdie
wi a puckle leaves,
is blawn richt ower the kirk steeple.
John Bell walks straucht through
the shut gates o' Pittendreigh Park,
never heard tell again an naebody speirs why?

SCOTS BARD

He wis taakin his breeks aff
when the thocht cam
in til's heid he
wad scrieve
a beeootiful pome

in English o' coorse.

SCOTS HAIKU
On the completion of the Scottish National Dictionary

Noo a' thae words
are in their tomb
whan will be
the resurrectioun?

URN BURIAL
(R.I.P. Scots Tongue)

It wis hardly worth peying for
a casket,
the body wis that peelie-wallie,

nae bluid in't
luikit like a
scrap o' broun paper

papyrus mebbe?
nae gran eneuch
for that,

but there wis some gran mourners, the
Editor o' the Scottish National Dictionary,
Heid o' the Depairtment o' Scot. Lit.,
President o' the Burns Federation,
President o' the Lallans Society,
President o' the Saltaire Society,
a' present in strict alphabetical order
an'
ane/twa orra Scot. Nats.

Syne cam a fuff o' win
an' liftit it oot o' the bowlie
an' hine awa,

a wee bird sang.

Dew dreep'd
on the beld heids
o' the auld men
stude gloweran
at the tuim tomb.

'She's jinkit again,
the bitch!'
said the man wi' the spade.

CAMELIAS IN THE SNAW
A compliment for Duncan Glen

It's a fair tyave, Duncan, 'gweed kens' (my nait'ral speak)
'foo ye dee it', forever drawing blooms frae thrissles
oot o thae ingrates, wha mak black merks on a white sheet,
while ootside their wee windaes the rain pooers doon —
gien veracity tae the pathetic fallacy — aa them,
hine awa in the country o the Bens and Glens
in the clean air, or so they like tae think o Scotland,
while pitten oot the cat, an the nearby Public Incinerator
spewing intae the cessile air black flakes o snaw
tae fa gently on oor heids at Canonmills. The while
y're haudin thegither thae swalt heids, wha think
genius rins oot their pens, an his wha flee aff the hanle
at ae breath o cauld reason, wha bite the haun
that offers malt, aye double malts, forbye.
Nae doot ye dae't in hope, a blinkin hope that yet meth oot
at ony moment, but wheesht! Your lugs aye cockit
for some richt soun that still taks up a truth
lang syne incorporate in word and act, and still
in spite o cheenge, stramash and deleterious talk,
is there — an if it's there you'll print it.
An whiles, God anely kens frae where your 'whiles' are come,
you're pitten word gin word yersel, sometimes nae mair
than notin the 'braw bress-haunled coffin' or mindin
'corrieneuchin aa the evenin' but in that honest settin doun
and in the thocht, abune, ablow, aboot the thing,
the haill climactic speaks — wanhope an mair's in the yokan
o wit an' word an' deed an' lovingkindness.
There's mair than meets the blindit ee that gabs:
'nae use, nae use, it's ethnic, Scots', nae sensing
the sweet haven tae which word an thing sooms in.
When I was boy I used tae watch a skeely man
stand easy, hands in pooches, on a slopin deck,
that near the slappin water that I thocht
the boat would coup. Nae odds tae him the heavin swall,
his boatie ran on the rhythm o ocean as she slipt
doon frae the heicht o the wave intae auld Faithlie's basin.
The picter bides, cam back tae me three years sin noo
in Arizona, when oot ahint a muckle desert rock
in mornin sun, black abune the lang horizon line,

distinct in yon clear air, I saw a rider, slow an easy,
movin on till oot o sicht; syne cam evenin licht
he's back movin as gentle as the boat rocks in calm sea.
Watchin that skeely body, legs an thighs pliant
tae the saft sides o her, his haill body swack, I lookit close —
'Nae saddle!' He tellt's he'd come gey near a thoosand mile.
His reid mustang was thrawn and jibbed at bit,
would hae nae leather wechts on's flesh, but took the man.
I saw him gin that big, tuim sky and that bare land —
waur nor Scotland.

Something atween man and boards o boat and watter,
something atween man and beast and yirth
worked for, waited for, in good hairt, was richt.
And sae it is wi his in words an line.
Yet something mair's required, some extraordinar jump.
This past December in Edinburgh toun,
I saw in snaw camelias bloom.

CRAFTSMAN

His being is at the pace
given by stone, wood, clay
to wrists, hands and fingers,
nor may be moved from this.

The world blazes and cries,
is shattered. He puts his hand
on clay, stone, wood,
or writes words to stay,

while the stone stars stay.

TREE

Drives down into night
as it drives up to day.
Men are no different,
lose one, lose all.

All those dancing candles
burning their white lights
are accountable to earth,
as men grow in love from it.

Highrising for stars
knowing but concrete underfoot
he will drive a stake
through your brain.

Each day puts a foot on earth.
Each day puts a hand to a star.

GANNET

The universe is made for gannets
or the gannet for its universe —
air and sea, a bolt from the blue, a model
so modified for its purpose to kill fish
as to be maximum, machine efficient — a response
in air to the given. Given fish in water;
given gannet, high, sky high, its gimlet eye
sees fish. Six-foot wing span moves, just,
into the wind's breath, faultless, hesitates,
interrupts its plane, shuts wing and plummets
from blue into that black, a single rhythmic
movement, predestined, as the bill strikes
hard water, to kill, and will emerge
into the sun as if he was a god's angel,
feathered only for beauty of flight,
a creation of the innocent eye, purposeless
other than to be a gannet in heaven.

WHY THE POET MAKES POEMS
(written to my dentist, Dr K P Durkacz
to explain why I failed to keep an appointment)

When it's all done and said
whether he is smithing away by the mad sea,
or, according to repute, silvering them in a garret
by moonlight, or in plush with a gold nib,
or plain bourgeois in a safe bungalow with a mortgage,
or in a place with a name, Paris, Warsaw, Edinburgh,
or sitting with his heart in the Highlands,
or taking time off at the office to pen a few words,
the whole business is a hang-over from the men in the trees,
when thunder and sun and quake and peas in a pod
were magic, and still is according to *his* book, admitting
botany is O K for the exposition of how the buds got there,
geology for how the rocks got just like that,
zoology for the how of the animals,
biology for us kind — but that's not his game:
he's after the lion playing around with the lamb for fun.
He doesn't want to know the how, the why. It's enough
    for him to say:
'That's what's going on. The grass is jumping for joy,
and all the little fishes are laughing their heads off.'

EARTH SANG

A tune rins in my heid this nicht,
I canna tell't.
That it should soun an' nae be tell't
An' yet aye felt
Like that sma soun that bides in shell
An' willna oot —
But deid it stops at the shell's mooth —
Bird an' sea soun, air reeshle in tree,
Thud o' hairt and yon big orchestra
That blaws, clood free, free farin,
An' that bairn soun that's naethin
But for the mither's ear an' then awa
Like fuff, 's as queer as bein here.

GLOSSARY

airn iron

ben maist inmost
bleat stupid
bleeze blaze

connach'd finished
coost cast
corrieneuchin conversing intimately
coup overturn

ee eye
een eyes
elbuck elbow
ettled purposed

Faithlie Fraserburgh
flooers flowers
foozlin overcoming
fuff puff of wind

gabs chatters
gawk stare idly

heilster gowdie head over heels
hine awa far away
his us

ingans onions
ingrates ungrateful people

jinkit dodged

lang syne long ago
loups leaps
lowe glow
lumpen soulless mass

mell't mingled

neeps turnips

oot out

peelie-wallie sickly, feeble
pit-mirk darkness
pooch pouch
puckle few
puir poor

quine girl

reeshle whistle

saps bread soaked in milk,
            childrens food
sarks shirts
sclimman climbing
shuin shoes
siller silver
skeely skilful
sonsy buxom
sooms swims
soon't sounded
souk suck
sproot sprout
stane stone
stookies stucco
stramash commotion
strang souch strong breathing
stravaig to make wander
swack supple
swall swell
swalt swollen
syne then

tatties potatoes
thrawn obstinate
tuim empty
tyave hard labour

virr vigour

wuids woods
wyte wait

yird, yirth earth